Some Words for Meanwhile

Lucia Galloway

FUTURECYCLE PRESS

www.futurecycle.org

Cover painting, "East River Park" by William Glackens; author photo by Judith Terzi; cover and interior book design by Diane Kistner; Georgia text and Bodoni Sans titling

Library of Congress Control Number: 2019940598

Published by FutureCycle Press
Athens, GA, USA

ISBN 978-1-942371-77-9

For John

Contents

I

II

III

IV

So many of the words are for meanwhile.

—Jack Gilbert

I

Home it turns out is more often elsewhere than not.

—Martha Ronk

Half-Moon

Out of fog melt,
sun-freeze

crisps crystalline edges
of hill and leaf,

inscribing
their syntax, their diction.

Last night's harvest moon
shows one ragged edge,

an erasure

and soon
only half of it.

When Warhol Sat for Alice Neel

after Neel's portrait of Andy Warhol in the Whitney Museum

From neck to abdomen
she renders flesh and bone, realizing in light and shadow
the sensuous, angered flesh, the bone, and muscles' tension,
swells and hollows of the torso,
flaps of slack or still-taut skin.

Did she ask to paint his scars—
those sinuous tracks across his chest
like railroad lines converging on his heart
laid open to the surgeons
who had massaged it with their hands?

I cannot turn away, much as I would like
to shrink from what seems shameful:
bizarre incision, surgical corset, sagging breasts.
I want instead to focus on the head and face—
its nose and unapologetic cheekbones, disdainful mouth,
deep cleft of chin. At first I do not even notice
that the eyes are closed.

Turquoise

Traded at Turkish bazaars to merchants en route
across the continent, the sky-blue gem from Persia rose
to prominence in Europe where, if legend tells us true,
it took its name, *turquois,* from the site
where sandaled traders dug in dusty toes.
Does this make turquoise ours?
I like believing that the Anasazi, skilled at quoits,
eager in the turquoise trade, also prospered in that quest,
thriving in our canyons until adversity came to rout
them. Quiet hues of sky and water filled a seam, suture
in the rock of a deeper tier. From this ground the osier
drew its drink. Ancient rites
paid homage to gods of what seemed sure,
that water would run and the sun would rise.

Traveling Alone in Assisi

1.

Light bisects narrow lanes
when morning throws itself
against signs and legends posted
on walls at street corners.
There is a saint whose city this once was.
Now the city owns the saint—
Francis, who turned from
sure entitlement to cast
his blessing on the birds
and make himself a life
among the poor.
There must have been a moment
when he feared he could not
compass this strange journey,
stranger to himself, winding through
narrow streets, turning corners
opening onto vistas dazzling
in new light. All this
Giotto and his lackeys
captured in wet plaster.

2.

Bare feet on cobbles
meant closer to God, and Francis
suffered on his once-sound leg
a suppurating wound
from the *stigmata*
that would not heal.
Clare sewed a sock to cover it,
made him a soft shoe

so he could go about the city—
the city that now owns Clare as well:
the dimly lighted cases
where, on display, the linen alb
and woolen cloak she wore
on errands to the poor.
Her bones rest in the crypt
of Santa Chiara, its outer walls
of Subasio limestone pink
and creamy white in the slanting sun.
I could die here
in this city of earth and ether.
Offer my flesh and bone
to be housed here,
slowly dissolve
under stone the color of
shells or the soles of
children's feet.

Architecture

for J.W.

Received your watercolor sketch, *plein air,*
the colonnade! Arches in burnt sienna,
pinkish brown, greenish grey—I've lost their
paint-tube names—spring from the top of a centered
capital. A sunlit triangle flares,
that burnished wing at the quoin,
the notch from which the arches vault
in opposite directions,
bent bows humming with their tonicity,
branches on their way to bower.

Bearing their weight, the trunk, a massive pillar:
greys and browns, greens that lean
toward blue laid down in watery strokes. Yet a
presence of sand and rock pervades: hints of jade,
of craggy shadow over restless sea.
Sun-glow, a centered streak, extols the column's mass.
This mineral light of water, earth, and air:
light that believes in architecture
believes as much in me, in you, distilling
our inmost seas and skies to moment.

Dazzle

for C.D.

After that cliff-hung moment,
after the mica's glint, the taste of snow,
when the birds had lapsed into silence,
when they clung to winter-brittle branches,
their summer nests long stolen...
Then you unfurled your wings, wove among clouds.
Then you scattered feathers that we might yet find
in your fledgling ascent
a place to stay.
And soaring above our alabaster loss—winsome,
gorgeous—you dazzled us.
And beauty complete
was bittersweet.

Conversation at Night

Bordering a walk between two buildings was a low wall where we sat in a ring of light to have the conversation we'd agreed to. To talk it out. Low wall beside a walk between two buildings, your shiny bicycle just there. In front of us while we had the conversation we'd agreed to. People walked by, glanced at us in our conversation, dodged the bicycle—its fat tires. Under the light, were we like boxers circling each other in the ring? Were we dancing partners wheeling warily, listening for the end of the last reprise? These are tired metaphors not up to figuring what we felt or said. What anybody saw. Everybody saw the bicycle—its fat tires. That frame, those spokes and tires: these alone were witnesses to what went down that night beside the walkway in the ring of light.

On Being Here

In the dream of white ground, black trees, blue dazzle
In the reality of soot-flecked slush under dishwater sky
In the loss of your favorite ring in a snowball fight
and the florist-stall daisies blue or magenta when you wanted white
In *Good morning* and *How are you?*
In the snatch of tango from the door of a bar
In the loofa, bath towel, and Kiehl's Coriander Lotion
In loons' call from the lake and the loose *v* of the mallard's wake
In calico carp kissing the surface of the botanic garden pond
and half a dozen hens scratching, swallowing grubs in their yard
In a month-old calf grazing pasture near its mother
In its dull-eyed destiny, forced to gorge on corn
In the ear of a weanling pig and the breath from a horse's nose
In the way you listen as carefully to the kitten's meow
as you listen to the questions of your children
here find the bedrock thrusting through the scree—
the children, small whistles piercing thicknesses of air.

Banking the Fire, a Fable

*Medieval legend has it that Saint Lucia
took out her own eyes to discourage
a persistent suitor who admired them.*

To carry them before her on a platter, her eyes
gouged out by her own hand, dismemberment

become a legacy, as if some inner voice were
whispering *Lucia, Lucia:* a mesmerism, trance.

And so this girl child reinvents herself as
Susie, child of *Punk* and *Africa*—their

dalliance in dappled tree-light where apples fall.
Punk, the ember-stick lighting the world's

sustaining fire; Africa, radiant with the spectrum
of tribes and nations. Miss SusieQ, she craves

the shimmering world. Sets out walking
down the street, announcing her departure

"on vacation." Not *vocation:* nothing so somber
calls—nor saintliness by its less hallowed names.

She shimmies into womanhood shedding her sparks
where they may fall. And, when she's menaced,

banks her fire, becomes the sun-warmed apple,
igneous: the fire's afterglow in stone.

Prairie Madness

Those years, a buck an hour to walk the aisles
of cornfields yanking tassels off the stalks.
Picked up by the captain's truck, half-bored,
I hustled, ignored the pollen—a workday script
of spunk and lunch-bag Twinkies my defense
against the possibility that I might well go mad.

I craved movie glamour, the storied mad-
cap rush of head-over-heels that ends in aisles
of churches. White gown, a guy beside: defense
enough against a rumor-horde that stalks
a teenage bride. *Children, obey your parents* (Bible script);
the parents: *Don't you dare claim you're bored!*

At fifteen, I thought surely an evil worm had bored
into Grandmother's brain, making her mad
and scared. *They're listening, waiting:* her demented script,
while my mind swam with images of aisles
of party dresses at the department store that stocks
the shortest shorts. Could these be my defense?

For sure, my closed bedroom door was no defense
against the voices of uncles, aunts, and in-laws, bored
with tears, who just that afternoon threw stalks
of lilies into Grandma's grave, her mind no longer mad,
they said, in death's goodbye. Then in the aisles
of night they leaked their ire into a grudging script,

raising the question of who would script
a letter to the State in Grandma's and their defense:
how much, if anything at all, those sterile aisles
of the asylum wards (her source of bed and board
for years) were worth in cash. Wouldn't it be mad
to pay the State for fodder—its dry stalks?

In my dreams, a phantom cornfield of colossal stalks
that shelter me, a sunburned kid trying to parse a script
worthy, almost, of Tennessee Williams—his mad
folk. Sanity is life's big compromise. Defense
is a conversation of the Angry to ensnare the Bored.
Life, a speeding train, the mind lurching in the aisles.

Would I be bored eventually among the stalks?
Yearn for a script beyond and west of mad?
A leafy defense, like flags afloat in aisles.

Dry Arroyos

This is a climate of summer weather
where caked earth cracks and grasses scorch.
This is a sky where no clouds gather.

Morning sun invades the screened-in porch.
Shadows shrink, the frail shade quivers.
Where caked earth cracks and grasses scorch,

lizards scud along the dusty rivers,
our dry arroyos, the tumbled stones.
Shadows shrink, the frail shade quivers.

Long evenings' cathedral light atones.
High noons glare, but supper-talk rebounds.
Our dry arroyos, the tumbled stones.

The heady darkness settles, interval that bounds
both dusk and dawn. Old women understand
high noons' glare, but supper-talk rebounds.

Night finds its legs. Coyotes band.
This is a climate of summer weather,
both dusk and dawn. Old women understand
this is a sky where no clouds gather.

Meanwhile: Visions & Dreams

1.

One summer evening when croquet games were common, a boy is sent to bed for sullying the grown-ups' play with his crying. He dreams of peacocks. He is a bantam rooster who can cross a lawn densely packed with peacocks only by passing through the spaces between their legs, much as wooden balls cross under the wickets of a croquet court. Wickets were, in fact, no foes to Charles and Emma Darwin, who kept on tapping and stroking their way around the court in the best of form. And Charles in his erudition knew that worms and insects, deep in the grass, find passages and arches essential to their own game—wickets of survival, wickets of chance. *I want to feel my toes in the grass,* the boy thinks, waking.

2.

Winter mornings, women find satisfaction ladling mush into bowls, placing them on the table with pitchers of milk. Circus posters cling in faded tatters to the barn wall. Turtles hibernate in mud beneath the freezing pond while, on its banks, squirrels and rabbits leave their tracery of tracks. Somewhere a woolly mammoth lies buried in a glacier. One special day a woman's piano is hauled on a dray-sled across the frozen landscape. In her chilly parlor, a child is building a ship on wheels.

3.

He sees and doesn't see her: pallid face in a drift of pillows; then a box moving away from him, hidden in the horse-drawn carriage that trundles ahead into indefinite dusk. Shaped as a box, she had become an alien thing going jiggety-jag down steep porch steps with six black-suited men.

He sees her tall again, lithe and rustling, her skirt awhirl with the falling light as she fetches him home from Yokum's place where, shooting his spit-shined marbles into a dirt-drawn ring, he'd overstayed his leave. Noisily, crowing with insult, he sprints homeward ahead of her scolding song.

Toes in the Grass

The tent stands over freshly mounded earth;
the lifts and small collapses of its canvas
breathe with the wind. Little flapping sounds remind
mourners that their lungs still work
inside bodies shaped like grief: overcoats
tenting bone, still-tethered hearts.

Beneath the awning, a boy stands breathing in
a bird-wing way, a stir of departure and flyway
open in his chest, sky thickening, clouds banking
stores of rain. Nothing he can know as loss-of-Mama
except, perhaps, the cold inside his shoes,
toes in the grass at the pit's brink.

Grass is another canopy. Weeds nestle—
little rooted tents of heart-shaped leaves.
Mallow and purslane: the boy will find them
in his own backyard. Even the gold dandelion
he will not pity, but give its rosette a yank,
until it comes up dirt and stem, taproot bared.

II

...most worthwhile pleasures
on this earth slip between gratifying another
and gratifying oneself.

—Maggie Nelson

Steelies

Taffeta sky   daft bees   marbles.
And what had seemed a well-worked plot
is fallow ground, ready for this story.

Cat's Eye, onyx. I draw my circle in the dirt.
Always you are indoors, Mother, sewing.
Steady feet work the treadle

heel to toe, flickering,
driving a rapier point
through layers of cloth.

The straight-away of long seams lets you speed ahead,
needle whistling ditties. But circles   of   sleeve holes,
collars   slow   you.   The needle labors, muttering

gingham,   muslin   cousins
I keep your cousins' names, Mom, from your stories:
Mabel   Earl   Harold   Jacob   May   and   *Laura*

names with oily surfaces,
cirrus swirls of white and yellow
round their roly-poly centers.

I have my aggies, alleys, steelies, turtles.
I'm knuckling down,
aiming my taw into the ring.

Come out,
see my dirty knees. Stitch me
into the circle of your story.

Like a Blossom

Papa used to get so mad, Mom said as she was driving,
*he'd grab the butcher knife and chase my mother through
the rooms, out into the yard, around the chicken house and barn.*
Beside Mom in the car's front seat, I squirmed and turned away.
I'd never seen a man unleash his rage.

My own dad was steady as a clockface,
lawn mower pusher, bringer-home of groceries,
block captain for blackouts the early years of war until, drafted,
he rode through France in jeeps with toothpaste, soap, cigarettes,
and ammo for troops.

Those years with Dad away, Mom's frustration a tight bud
I was just old enough to notice that cold spring of 1944:
her ration coupons, lonely bed—I see it now—the scattered crayons,
chapped knees, two kids with snotty noses. She'd run outside,
break switches off the willow, cut the air.

Like a daffodil, my mom. Spring flower whose stem gyrates
in a gale. Fins along its length let the blossom turn its head
and bend instead of break.

Homage to Style

for the women of the 1940s

It was a talent she didn't recognize—
this posing in the sunlit yard
for the black-box Brownie,
a predilection of the bones
as she eased arms tired from ironing
or smearing packets of orange dye
into blocks of lard-like oleo—
eased them into a dress
with a yoke that fit snug over the hips
and skirt that flared in shapely gores
to just below the knees.
No crime is so great as daring to excel,
said Churchill. And she *was* criminally inclined,
as much as the waitress
behind Woolworth's lunch counter
in the yellow cotton uniform, her hair
in a snood to keep stray strands
out of the blue-plate special.
*It is fun to be in the same decade
with you,* said FDR to Churchill, though he might
as well have tossed his small bouquet
to the woman who met the troop train
in her smart coat, her shoes with open vamps,
who saved the cost of precious hose
by wearing liquid makeup on her legs
instead of stockings. *Remember,
you are just an extra in everyone else's play,*
said Roosevelt. But Churchill said,
*To improve is to change,
to be perfect is to change often.*

Renditions

1.

In Warsaw, chandeliers and molded chairs—
the blonde wood's modern, midtown setting.

Outside, waiting for Mass to finish,
we pose for photos beside our concert poster:

Chorale to sing at 4:00
Music of American composers

Our bright sound issues like the pulse of rain
to thunderous applause: the roar of an express train

rushing past the crowd on a station platform.
That quickly, our first performance is complete.

Jubilant, our conductor, perspiring in his tux,
accepts a box of candy. We unzip each other's

dresses, shrug them off sweaty shoulders,
stuff their black polyester into backpacks.

Prepare to breeze down Warsaw's fashionable streets
in search of restaurants and wine.

2.

In Krakow, the Conservatory at 3:00, we climb
three flights to a stifling classroom at the top,

throw open French doors to a balcony.
Men remove tuxedo jackets.

White looks cooler, and we women yearn
to hang our dresses on the wall pegs,

sing in pearls and panties,
putting aside long skirts.

Displeased, our conductor sends us to the balcony
to drink bottled water while our Polish audience

fills the chairs, the aisles. Some sit cross-legged
on the floor. We omit "Lamentations of Jeremiah"

from our program: no such bombast for this vesper crowd!
Filing back onto the balcony to an uproar of applause,

we lift skirts, raise underarms to faint breezes,
take photos of a formal garden below.

3.

In Tarnow, we splurge on ice cream sundaes
while the sky darkens, while waiters tie awnings,

drag chairs and tables from the patio
into dim interiors. A heavy storm predicted.

Arriving at our concert venue as the sky opens,
singers scurry, opening umbrellas, to a change of clothes

in the Rectory. Men dress first while our conductor
ascends to a top floor aery to wash up, don in privacy

tuxedo, coat and tails. Impatient women change
inside the bus while the parking lot fills, and church pews:

men, women, and children, a group of Polish singers
in peasant dress. At concert's end, we recess down the aisle,

clasping with one hand parishioners' outstretched hands,
holding in the other long-stemmed white roses

we'd been given moments before as the applause
swelled the vaulted ceiling of the church's nave.

4.

That afternoon, touring the old city with a guide,
we'd felt the presence of the cast-out Jews:

a plaque and remnant from what
had been their synagogue, there off the main square

where inside the old Tarnow Cathedral
we'd paused to sing spontaneously

a rendition of Ron Kean's *Kyrie*—
Ron Kean, composer of *our* sacred music,

himself a Jew. Did I think then of the trip
our group would make as tourists the next morning?

Singers who knew no anthems for Auschwitz,
its mounds of worn suitcases, loose balls of

human hair, trash heap of wire eyeglass frames.
We had no harmonies for Birkenau—

its rows of toilets, rank straw pallets—I can scarcely
say it, though I see it still.

Cochineal

How we set ourselves apart. How we projected, as halo,
blood and fire, signatures of our humanity. Found a coal
in the mineral-laden earth to make a line
of dyes from hematite, from cinnabar, and color with lean
bright orange our capes and winding cloths. How the ache
in us persisted like a hunger for some choice
not yet presented, for a hue that we could hail
as shout, not merely tolerate as echo.
Here is a chain of story: how we came to cinch
our grandeur, display in triptych and tunic our élan.
How, fortunate, we found the color crimson that had lain
as pigment in tiny parasites that etched a kind of lace
on pads of nopal—that cactus wild and hale
in Mexico, Peru. These insect bodies found their niche
as lading in Spanish ships, traded across an ocean.
How cochineal red became the *crepe de Chine*
of many merchants' ventures. As if the ail-
ment of our evanescence would surely heal
if only we had, of red, sufficient cache.

Tomatoes

At 6:00 the greenish sky, taupe, purple as a cape,
looses its torrents amidst crash and splintering and is spent.
Our shadows drenched, dissolved. Still I thrill to see these
orange and crimson swords pierce the loitering cloudbank.
Mother, I wait for you to wield your dripping lance.

Candles center the table, afloat in your crystal bowl.
Flames waver from the waxen boats, cast trapezoids
and secret triangles upon the water. Your tomato wheels layer
a plate, their clean-sliced surfaces like lambent moons
in a cloud-tailed sky. Our one moon rises.

Sky had hung, heavy as a clothesline sheet.
Wind had gusted, loam in the nose, a sudden chill.
Something of rain and wind clings to these tomatoes shining
on their plate, clear as an evening transparent with release.
Pairs of lungs in their cut surfaces. Water wings that let us float.

You have mortified the tempest. You, Mother, old regulator
of clouds: your tomatoes our almanac, our tidal chart.

Something in Me Wanting to be Bad

Upside-down on monkey bars, skirt around my head
and panties flaming, I spiral down
the fire escape's dark tunnel, kick
the teacher who catches me as I shoot into light.

Once I made a corps of paper dolls
from cardboard backs of writing tablets.
Blonde hair curled at their napes. They wore pink underwear,
red slippers, or stilettos. Gail's were much like mine, but uglier—
small waists, thick legs, black boots. Their garter belts
and bustiers seemed Amazonian, and their eyebrows,
arched and heavy, menaced their small faces.
I threw them into a mud puddle and dared her
to ask about them—favorites she'd lent,
wanting me to make them clothes.

Find those paper dolls, I wouldn't. Could not have,
anyway, paper and water what they are.
This story's telling finds me in the trap I set.
The Amazon I vanquished voodoos me, miniskirted,
in dark tights and boots. Slim camisoles for cleavage
and bare arms. But kick-ass desires must now find guise
in wit, words to show there's fire yet.
A whip, a scourge even, to draw blood.

I Read into David Hockney's Painting

after Hockney's "My Parents"

They don't like the chairs on which they sit—
modern, uncomfortable, not what they are used to.
These chairs seem hardly chairs at all, in profile like
short stepladders, each parent like a can of paint
perched on one of those wobbly, protruding shelves.

It's not as though they don't cooperate, positioned
on either side of a small cabinet rolled in
like a substitute for the kitchen table.
Mom's an upright presence, hands clasped demurely in her lap,
knees and toes touching
so that her legs bow in a tight parenthesis
that contains her disappointment I haven't married handsomely.
She's forbearing in blue, a gentian reservoir.
Dad's position threatens
to overturn his rig. He bends forward, tenses
his arms and legs, and lifts his heels,
revealing steely sock tops under umber trousers.
He's poring over an atlas open on his knees, dreaming
his trip around the world, willing not to think about me
living on the Coast and
taking up with hippies.

Poised between tension and release, the parents
make their ladders tremble.
Mother declines to crochet (because there is no baby).
And Father: maybe it's the family album
he leafs through trying to forget that I am not—and never have been—
any good at tennis.

Meanwhile: Occasions & Notions

1.

Things call out, eliciting answers of duty or desire. Women look for outing flannel, muslin, gingham, satin ribbon, Putnam Fadeless Dye. The vinegar barrel boasts a wooden pump, the coffee mill two giant wheels. Beside flat boxes of Star and Horseshoe chewing tobacco sits a guillotine with stained and sticky blade. The candy man arrives at C. E. Sperry & Co with his sample case that opens to form a valley, metal trays of caramels stepping up its sides. Boys in black ribbed stockings crowd around to ogle lemon and chocolate drops, licorice lozenges, peppermint wheels, and gumdrop jewels like dusty cabochons. *No other day like this. Sweets! You may choose just one.*

2.

A four-room house where a little boy lives with his mama and papa is eased from its foundation, loaded with block and tackle onto a flatbed truck, and set down in a new yard among different neighbors. Down-to-earth, these folk. No one marvels that not a drop of water spilled from the bowl on the wash stand. They're having a bowl shower for the dear woman who complains she never has enough for beating eggs and mixing cakes, for serving chowder and steaming mush. The boy imagines bowls falling from the sky. Sometimes he thinks about the cyclone: hail and rain, the outhouse overturned and hollyhocks bent double. How the next morning he went with his papa to inspect the rubble of strewn planks and uprooted trees—massive root bowls umber with clinging dirt.

3.

Once, in an overheated church, a boy had clasped his friend's hand tightly as they went forward for the altar call. That day he had ruined his clothes crashing through thin ice into a muddy river at the bottom of the hill where he was sledding. All afternoon he sat in the classroom in his brown-stained union suit while jacket, shirt, and trousers hung drying by the schoolroom stove. He mashed his brush in a pot of water and in a pot of paint, muddying his paper like the coattails of the circuit preacher, like the cloaks of evangelists since the founding of Christendom who must wait for warmer weather to resume the baptisms of the converted. A river will serve. So will the shallow waters of a farmyard pond. The boy will remember only this: the heat of the June morning and the scratch of hay in the barn where he stripped off his sodden clothes.

At water's edge, mosquitoes knot the air with their rasping whine.

Living Room

Sauntering among table legs, beneath dining chairs,
an arpeggio of legs, the cat has entered,
announcing herself.

At her level, petals' hues deepen toward
their centers—sculpted flowers on the Chinese rug.
Branches, leaves etch troughs through tufted wool.

Too much about legs, our decorator says:
your several tables, your Bechstein grand above
that vacant forest floor. The cat devours a bird,
scattering its feathers. Kids play with Legos, losing the tiles.
They picnic; they camp out.

But we are adamant. Just look at the piano keys,
bass clef and treble, ivories grimed and gritty
with the detritus of our sloughing off.

We lean in, press and caress, straddling the chords,
riding the arpeggios, those lyric flights.
We play it out.

Love's Supper

after the first line of Neruda's "Sonnet XXIII"

The fire for light, the rancorous moon for bread:
There is a window, lattice of small panes
that mirrors our bone-picked supper, fractured
in the indigo, branch-cluttered night.

Birds in their roosts: from flight, uneasy rest.
Leaves curl on flagstones, mute contorted fists
that cannot say, *O love, what is your wish?*
We've half again as much to say as we have said.

Set down the goblet, and the carmine wine
sheets down its sides to pool in the bowl.
Let's drink the words instead of hoarding them.

Ourselves, we are the bitter Eucharist—
crumbs of dry loaves, the orts and crusts
that must be consumed or scattered in the wild.

To the Piano

Aristocrat
out of forests, savannahs,
semitropic jungles:
sunlight and rain
wove the grain
of your case.
An elephant's honed instincts
congealed
your ivory-slippered
keys.

Like opening an atlas,
I lift your heavy lid.
Inside the chamber
of your strings
a widening river,
that ancient bridge in Budapest
across the Danube.
What thunder
lurks
in those felted hammers
quiet in repose?

Although
you host photographs
as if your surface
were a mantelpiece,
edict holds that
coffee cups,
wine glasses,
vases of cut flowers
shall not
rest there.
Hubby has spoken,
and yet he humors
your cousins
less meticulous:

that jazzy upright
in a New Orleans bar,
riffs wafting
like gumbo's aroma,
complex and fishy,
with bourbon
hinting its sweet, stringent
notes
and wisteria
round a wrought iron balcony
overhanging
a dark street.
The ballet-school piano,
powder blue
in a Chelsea flat,
tired hammers and strings
tainted with sweat,
the worn-out toe shoes,
the endless
pirouette.

My piano,
you are truly grand,
a flying elephant,
one ear
flapping.
I want to be
tucked up
in your curled trunk,
relieved
of cynicism,
staving off imperatives,
in the comfort
of your
well-seasoned hide.

In Your Midnight Kitchen

you heap peeled garlic in the scale's basket—
a dozen cloves or more, like giant water pearls,
a reverence in your handling like Aladdin's, rubbing
the quiescent lamp. And when you've got the genie,
a kind of servant-alchemist,
you're ready for the transmutation, chemical and aromatic,
of garlic pulverized with emollient oil,
spiked with vinegar and mustard,
and bound with an egg.

Aioli, pungent custard gold.

And here is what we know: that *alliinase,* an enzyme,
neighbors a compound, *alliin:* these two held chaste
in separate cells. But when the clove's cell walls
are breached *with crushing, chopping, slicing. biting;*
then (and only then) springs forth *allicin,* garlic's secret
and its chief allure.

It is a violence I can sing:
Aladdin, alchemist, allicin, aioli—this flutter of
exotic moths in the night kitchen
around your votive light.

The Legs for It

Rust rouges your fingertips and thumb
when you rub the circumference
of the cast-iron skillet you put away without drying.
Rust the color of war paint, of dried blood.

Some fruits don't ripen until they fall.
In the overheated kitchen you carve an avocado,
slice creamy crescents into a bowl of greens.
Here is no red in ripeness, no blood.

There's an old slimming diet of just red meat.

You have the legs for it:
for finishing triathlons, winning the broad jump.
Your swift backward kick slams shut the door,
your thighs flashing pale in dim light.

Rust rouges the fingertips and thumb.
There's an old slimming diet of just red meat.
Some fruits don't ripen until they fall.

Cooking with Garlic

Naked cloves I've just released
from their jackets clump on the cutting board,
dormant lanterns, their facets retaining heat
from my hand.

Look now: firefly in a vial,
in a teardrop.
Light, but no fire.

Whenever two cloves are called for,
remember to use at least four. Four is a family,
or five, roasted in a small clay casserole. Or chopped
and sautéed live in olive oil until they're straw-hued,
golden. In these we anticipate the sweetness of cashew;
the brio of fresh coffee, its hint of bitterness like filbert,
like walnut. There will be fine sensations
and tears in the house by night.

III

And every blossom on the bush
Adjusts its tumbled head—

—Emily Dickinson

For Girlhood

Near Albuquerque wild rains sweep mesas in the dark.
Satisfying, to drowse aboard the night train in the dark.

We cut a hole in the gazebo roof last summer, confident
that fireflies and starlight would remain in the dark.

Asters and watermelon lade the table on the old screen porch.
Outside, I hear the pump handle strain in the dark.

Norma in her plaid sheath is seated at the upright piano.
Does she wonder which overtures to entertain in the dark?

Lay the wild rose, violet, vetch, and shooting star between
the pages of the press their juices will stain in the dark.

Stars and space: the great galactic sieve too filigreed to hold
without the stuff of burnt-out stars, cohesive vein in the dark.

Hinged, in two parts, seemed the autumn moon one night—
the dangling capsule of a construction crane in the dark.

St. Lucy's Day, a crown of candles, coffee, saffron buns:
small fires an early morning can contain in the dark.

Celebrity

to our Moon of June 20, 2016

Pink, like the strawberries we ate in Kyoto
that March we visited—already sweet, and cool as
the snow on Mr. Fuji at sunset, Strawberry Moon.

Wikipedia photos find my screen. Some see
your ruddy face as I did: burnt red dwindling to
orange in the translucence of summer's first night.

Night that signaled the start of the strawberry picking
for the Algonquin. Night above ocean beaches
on Long Island, and here on L.A.'s parched shores.

I hope the sky was clear this night in Warsaw,
your radiance outdoing the clockface in the tower,
Stalin's Palace of Science and Culture.

I hope old women of the city gazed at you
recalling another June, 1948, the Rose Moon—
your moniker in Europe—when Warsaw lay,

a rubble of stones lining tank-rutted boulevards;
and over Auschwitz-Birkenau, emptied finally of its
populations, you mourned, I hope, those thousands.

Sun-ripened moon, I hope you glowed, roseate
in a cloudless sky this 2016 solstice in Warsaw,
reprising your appearance in blushing plums,

in tomatoes sliced in shining moons for tourists
next morning at Hotel Mercure's breakfast buffet.
Roses adorn the tables where women are opening

compacts in readiness for sightseeing and
being seen. What would you do, Moon, if *you* set
the agenda? If Sun were not at its highest while

you were at your lowest, indebted to Earth's
atmosphere for your cosmetic glow? Take a bow
while the credits roll. The gigs line up as

the planet twirls: Harvest Moon, Blood Moon.
Your alliance with Sun, with tethering Earth—
how long? How long will the planet last?

Chalcedony

What other matriarch bears a load
of such extensive progeny? Chance
named her after ancient Chalcedon.
Then, as favored stone for rulers' seals, she took the lead.
Cognomen for the fibrous quartz clan:
agate, carnelian, onyx, chrysoprase, heady
aventurine, green jasper, and heliotrope laced
with red or yellow. This lustrous family clad
Moses' brother in a breastplate of splendor and ado.
A jeweler's yen for beads and bezels honed
merchants' dreams, put caravans on every lane
of trade, while European carvers made from haloed
agate milky cameos. And when the lode
of local rock ran thin, merchants could lade
the holds of ships with agate from Brazil. O halcyon
years of intaglio, of Florentine *commesso*! Not cloyed,
although a tad complacent, these quartzes dance
through history—a fantasia, *un dolce.*

Impromptus on the Figure of a Fan

1.

Flounces, tassels,
bows and laces
all laid aside
along with
her folded fan,
she births him
from an oval belly
past seductive.

2.

Decorative like fringes,
her fingers on a chair arm.
When they curve around
a needle, a pebbled orange,
the corner of a book,
they draw forth
histories folded
like the inside of a fan.

3.

A fan unmans authority,
like the orange englobed
in pungent skin: opened
in wedges, it's a tease.
An orange like a woman's breast,
the map for which is
a folded fan.

4.

Noticing a fan looped
from her wrist,
a man may suffer
the barest disappointment
at its opening: tree trunks,
blossoms, sunlight,
those strolling figures
between its spines.

Eating and Other Disorders

The novice cook seeks Julia's expertise
for blanching to perfection *haricots*.
Mushy beans cannot but some displease.
Some gourmands love to eat raw cookie dough.

The infant sucks her own extremity;
the doting parents think it's all for show.
The babe—as if to say *Je vous en prie*—
she coos and savors yet another toe.

A rabbit in its hutch adores a pellet,
a hungry man craves steak straight from a skillet.
The bored resort to nibbling canned sardines.

I've guzzled noodles Taranto to Bangkok.
That *soupçon* of something earthy in the stock!
Quel aphrodisiaque? Quelles herbes fines?

Of Petrarch and Cigarettes

My thoughts are fresh today,
missing that sexy idyll
of flip-flops and bare legs
caressed by summer's sun.

Missing that sexy idyll
of Petrarch's Laura
caressed by summer's sun,
I smoked a fag, but still I think

of Petrarch's Laura.
Too much already.
I smoked a fag, but still I think
Petrarch. Is that sexy?

Too much already
about books and reading
Petrarch. Is that sexy?
Let's talk now of smoking.

About books and reading
generally, not enough is said.
But let's talk now of smoking
cigarettes, their glowing tips.

Generally, not enough is said
about the gift of cool white
cigarettes, their glowing tips.
(Don't even think of sex!)

About the gift of cool white
sheets, I'm fantasizing now,
not thinking, no! of sex.
My thoughts are fresh today.

What Mother Said

Burlesque. Just cheap burlesque!
that Betty Grable movie we saw,
When My Baby Smiles at Me.
Her Mennonite dismissal of the glitter, the risqué—
no stomach for it. Or was she aiming for sophistication
while chatting with the next-door neighbor,
a daily-use patina that reveals a certain class?
But this is grown-up thinking. Age nine, I wanted
Betty Grable on the runway, kicking high in heels,
silk stockings. Showing leg. Dazzling me with feathers, fringes,
as my fingers tried the arcs of Bach's arpeggios,
my dutiful exertion at the piano.
I claimed *burlesque* but knew it only like knowing
grass loves naked toes, or sin is *dark*
and sex is good for making babies.
Didn't know then about our hearts, their hundred-thousand beats
a day, our busy brains that register as many words—
every word a heartbeat. Mother would have shamed me
if she'd known. Known that I could own *burlesque.*
Known what the heart is good for.

Hosting the Duke at the Cotton Club, circa 1927

Never seen the club so jammed.
Not a dime-size spot out there
on the dance floor. What a mob!
A real Hades in Harlem!
What's that? Ah yes, little gal
at the ring-side table wants
us to play "Going to Town."

You there in the catbird seat!
Your dress hikes up a tad; you
cross one leg over the knee,
unfold it in the humid
dusk of the sidelines to tease
the toe of your dancing shoe
into the pool of cool light.

I own the night on this floor
where folks join "The Cotton Club
Stomp." Jungle music! Timid
of their shadows, if you ask
me, an emcee in garters
to hold up his socks while his
tuxedo flashes black, white.

How you people like to do
things, go places, see people!
Marvelous, the way you've all
warmed up to our little show!
I do love applause. Dukie
loves applause, whistles kisses.
So! "First We Freeze, Then We Melt."

We melt into reflections
in a Macy's plate glass pane.

The Whole Stock

The frequent flyer smokes her duty-frees,
breathes fantasies of fishing from a pier,
blows perfect smoke rings at the sommelier,
her wine a pale Chablis, her blouse cerise.

Recalling she had always been a tease,
her dandy beau, intrepid buccaneer,
sites her brave blouse, imagines a lace brassiere.
The mound of good occasions some unease.

They order sea bream, shallots, braised burbot,
even smoked shark on beds of bergamot.
On s'excuse, no whales today came back to dock.

Cetaceans' fins and flukes—their absent sheen,
a momentary dampness chills the scene.
Gone all: the prawns, the lobsters, the whole stock.

IV

Meanwhile the world goes on.
Meanwhile the sun and the clear pebbles of the rain
are moving across the landscapes,
over the prairies and the deep trees,
the mountains and the rivers.

—Mary Oliver

Some Words for Meanwhile

January 19, 2017

There is only this way,
this one way,
to breathe   while
rain falls—
finally falls and falls—
in Southern California.
Comes in repeated fits,
storms over parched lands
and lawns. Pools at our doorsteps
from overflowing gutters, sheets
off the pavements of parking lots,
carves new rivulets
in our gardens, our
paths and trails.

One way   while
crews erect viewing stands
in D.C.—mile after mile
of bleachers, media towers—
along the storied route.
While in airports, passengers
clutch boarding passes, eye
podium monitors.
While on basement floors,
at kitchen tables, women paint
slogans: *Resistance is Joy.*
Pack boots, mufflers
and down jackets.
D.C., Chicago, Tucson, Denver, L.A.
...(will the buses make it?)   while
they hope that nothing happens,
knowing that *nothing*
can mean *anything* now.

Migration

The calendar flaunts an oriole.
Forgotten are the indigo bunting,
the tern, the ring-billed gull—
all torn off, tossed in the bin.

A thesaurus nestles beside the rhyming dictionary
that whispers of weather and tether.

The paperweight is a sturdy bubble
awaiting the day the notes and reminders
take wing and fly in formation
to join the grand migration.

The calendar flaunts an oriole.
A thesaurus nestles beside the rhyming dictionary.
The paperweight is a sturdy bubble.
The bathrobe worries its wearer
over a stray feather in its pocket.

Where did it come from, and where
now is the bird that lost it?

Bunting with Birders

He cinches our little group in a lariat of scold:
Spit-spit-spit-spit. Moments ago he'd been an
indigo apotheosis captured, sunlit, in our scope.

Voyeurs and tricksters, we would fix upon
a way to lure him closer with a tape recording
of his territorial song. So now he circles us

to tell us off. What creature does not perceive
itself the center of the world? Unaware his plumes
entirely lack blue pigment, that light diffracted

through his feathers confers this eminence of being,
he goes about it: mating and hunting as if the world
depended on it. His is a story that's not a story—

motive only without conceit. And we, we're left
with theories of behavior and feather, sentences
outranking song—nothing, really, except conceit.

Apologia for Prayer

"If I should die before I wake..."

And it's not as though staying awake
will save you. Think of those things
outside even Jove's control:
the blast, the bullet,
the careening car,
funneling wind, voracious fire.
Think of Vesuvius spewing,
Pompeii's people silent, silted.

Like boarding a train,
prayer is homage to the leaping hour.
It follows then that prayers unsaid
are a dance refused,
a gift unsent or put away unused,
the soul's torpor on a hot afternoon
and no rain falling.

Barn Raising

Bye-bye, Miss American Pie.
—Don McLean

Waiters' ghosts still scurry at Windows on the World
while a hundred phantom farmers raise the beams,
striving in concert to bring up the frame
until they hear the clanging dinner bell.
Fifty pounds of roast beef and three hams,
three hundred light rolls, pickled beets.

A stand of trees in rural Indiana beats
the kitchen of a restaurant—chefs' world
among the clouds. Made-to-order ham
omelets for the CEOs? No one beams
approval. *Now why the Sam Hill's that bell
cutting like a buzz saw into morning's frame?*

The man who raised the barn still sees its frame.
Somewhere, the pilot of the plane remembers the beat
of his own heart and terror like a bell
ringing out the seconds of a world
contracted to the shimmer of a beam.
And he had scarcely time or space to ham-

mer home a thought of Grandmother's strong hams,
her floury hips brushing the door frame
as she fetched a hank of garlic from the beam.
Summer's harvest stores the same sun that beat
on the east-facing walls of the World
Trade Center towers. And the belle

of many balls at work in offices of Bell,
Hurd, and Houlihan will not see again the Hamp-
tons and their beaches, where she owned the world.
One-hundred-twenty lemon pies could frame
the ambitions of a rural wife. Does baking beat
basking in the aura of fluorescent beams?

The towers' upper strength relied on beams
resting on lower verticals, sound as a bell.
There's never been anything that beats
American resourcefulness: the Coke, ham-
burger and side of fries; the drive to frame
a formula to dominate the world.

As pie-shaped moons beam on a world
of Honey Baked Ham and Taco Bell,
pneumatic hammers beat new rivets into frames.

Frankincense

From scraggly trunks of the *Boswellia,* a resin
flows when those who seek it slash its skin.
It weeps, and tears solidify. Intrepid harvesters risk
danger from the venomous snake
living in those trees that eke
their life from sun and rock, but little rain.
How is it that with tears, with snake and knife,
we humans trace our shifts and turns? The making of a scar.
Charred *Boswellia* resin ground to powder, pressed to cakes
of kohl: Cleopatra wore the eyeliner—black ink
to inscribe an episode, the tale of Rome's imperial arc.
Matthew the gospel writer paints a different scene:
gifts borne from the East by men of rank—
congealed tears as homage to a baby born outside an inn.
Aromas balsamic-spicy, lemony, hinting of conifer sink
into the mesh of history. Along the Incense
Road from ancient Ubar, Franks
brought fragrant smoke to Europe's censer,
salve to souls and bodies weary from the race.

Modern Mom Views Raphael's
Madonna and Child with Book

Caught up in interplay of chubby fingers and
Madonna's slimmer hand, the aura cast by gilt-edged
pages on the baby's skin, Modern Mom can't give
the book itself a thought. She craves sensation.
Through the cushion on Madonna's lap, she takes in
heat of baby buttocks and plump legs. Envies,
almost, Madonna. Covets the filament, the tether
of that maternal gaze.

Entranced, she's tracing curves and ovals
in Madonna's face and the encircling hood. See how
its oval opening finds the column of her neck! And
here, the infant's cheek, a circle. Belly too, its navel
a tidy little oval of its own! (She doesn't see the book
as Raphael's device, a prop for disposing,
at center canvas, arms-wrists-knuckles-fingers.)

She lets herself luxuriate in faces. Madonna and son,
each face contains a triangle, two points the far corners
of their eyes, the third point touching shadows
beneath the lower lip. In Madonna's eyes, the base
of yet another triangle, its apex reaching downward to
the infant face, making their gaze a wedge-shaped ray.
Making our Mom believe it. Yet,

how fragile such a moment. How soon broken:
baby or mother drawn away by sudden noise,
an itch or hunger pang, a bird that settles on the wall behind.
Nothing left but turn again to the knot of palms and fingers
supporting the object mother and child are holding.
How can it be? This complicated play around a *book*.
A testament of life outside this moment.
Of Time itself. Of an unfolding.

Ten Miles from Home

The captain mans a joystick, flies a drone.
Through windswept desert, on H 85,
he drives an SUV to work 10 miles from home.

In his office-cockpit, he takes the Naugahyde throne.
He studies monitors that show the villagers alive.
The captain mans a joystick, flies a drone.

Vegas glitter and Nevada's barren stone
recede, along with barbeque and soccer, from lives
of men who drive to work 10 miles from home.

Almost audible, a cyberspatial moan
that follows *3-2-1, rifle!* and a missile's dive.
The captain mans a joystick, flies a drone.

Crumbs on the kitchen floor, a jangling phone—
he pulls himself away from his domestic hive
for duty in a land 10 miles from home.

He cites rewarding moments helping lone
compatriot ground crew near Kandahar survive.
The captain mans a joystick, flies a drone.
He drives an SUV to work 10 miles from home.

Meanwhile: Mimes & Ghosts

1.

In scarlet coats and white helmets, mounted bobbies regale Toronto's streets while Fall's abundance overspills its market stalls—squashes, bright apples, tawny peaches, wands of bittersweet like ember-sticks aglow. The visiting family slakes its thirst with fire, but the impatient son turns his head away at precisely the moment when a fake battleship sinks into Lake Ontario in a burst of sparks and flame. His grandmother has nicknamed her favorite household squirrel *Jellicoe* after an admiral defending the Empire on the North Sea. She hooks one thing to another with rows of stitches descending from her knitting needles. Dangling from shoppers' basket rims, limp necks of geese accuse—their beaks and lifeless eyes. Ghosts of smoke drift in the autumn sky.

2.

Boys begin to notice hieroglyphs on inside doors of toilet stalls. Doors have many uses, one of them realizes when invited to play a new game at a friend's twelfth birthday party. No longer just a surface for pinning a tail on the donkey, now it's a mysterious *post office* door with a letter waiting behind it. The boy is all aquiver. The winter past he'd had his nerves rattled at the conclusion of a wedding, only the second that he'd seen. From the snowy yard under the bedroom window came hoots and hollers, pan lids clanging, tin horns blatting, shotgun blasts. Finally, the bride's father threw open the front door and asked the bedevilers in, offering long cigars.

Now spring is sliding into summer. The post office is a new-leafed tree with a secret room where he has gone to get a letter. *Who sent it?* At first he does not want to open the strange envelope of leaves.

Elegance

This delicacy of weddings, Quinceañeras:
I've made almond cake for the homeless

who gather with us to dine on real, not
paper, plates, with stainless steel forks

and knives, places set out on tablecloths
accessorized with folded napkins,

bite-size chocolate kisses. This week
kernels of candy corn and grinning

jack-o-lanterns charm off autumn's chill.
Extravagant! I dread the verdict, muttered

or suppressed. Almonds. Even a man
without a home knows of the thirsty

almond trees, notorious in this time
of drought. Even he has read of growers

who pour a gallon of water into every nut.
I spent hours on the cake, soaking a pound

of almonds in more water overnight. And
these men on shelter cots shaking off

morning sleep while I am slipping each
kernel of its skin, tossing it on the pile

of nutmeats naked, ready to be ground
to meal. I'd walked the orchard aisles once,

watching automated arms clamp vice-like
fists around each tree trunk, shake until its

branches dropped full hulls along the rows,
where, forked up, they were whisked away

to quaking tanks, spewed through chutes
in the progressive nakedness of harvest.

Released, the inmost lode.
Released, the shell.

Released, the hull around the shell,
released, and filtered out, the rocks and twigs.

I place a coffee urn next to the cake, elegant
as an ice rink in its disarming sheen.

It's after that I overhear him—one of our
guests returning to the table with cake

and coffee. *Elegant,* he's saying. And then,
Our supper talk, the give and take of it:

community we miss, he says. *How long since*
we could afford the elegance of conversation?

This unexpected hallowing. I'm shaken.

Extra

Buttons: I'd snip the paper packets
from their hangtags, toss them into a box,
some three or four in a score of years
put to use, a number that to some
might seem absurdly small. But see,

I found a button to replace the one
my husband lost from his favorite sweater.
It is of molded plastic embossed with seams
to look like woven leather and has a sturdy shank
for two layers of wool and grosgrain facing. Not
a perfect match—

smaller than the others, tawnier.
This, the button in my box to do the job.

Dance Card

Old men of this town
hand us from our chairs
and we waltz, held
at arms' length, our
waists the stems of bouquets,
lips and lashes fragrant, floral.
Cadences swell into bloom.

Young men of this city
pick us off the wall
and we tango, our torsos
proud, feet in conversation.
Glissandos, pizzicatos like
the stems of roses held
between the teeth.

But old men, away!
It is late; we grow trite.
And you boys must not stay—
your wiles and your toys.

~~~

Oh but Gentlemen, wait!
Hidalgos, come back!
Chevalier, caballero,
come riding,
come striding back.

To Another Guest, After the Wedding

Witness with me the bride
launching her bunched gardenias
into the humid air, gathering
the cumulus of her heavy skirt
into the white limousine.

Let us smoke, disappearing
under a tree, unwinding pale skeins.
Two crones skin-dusted in mist
while high on their stems
turbines—those austere windmills—
like oracles, speak in signs.

Let us recall the car that carried us
to the ceremony and the car
we followed in the downpour,
how it dissolved in a cloud
of spray from the pavement,

how it appeared again, a ghost
materializing, and how we parked
beside it on the street beside the church
and, alighting, defined ourselves
with black umbrellas.

Notes

The book's opening epigraph is a Jack Gilbert quotation from "The Butternut Tree at Fort Juniper," found in *Refusing Heaven* (Alfred A. Knopf, 2005), p. 41.

Section I's epigraph comes from Martha Ronk's "Homesick," *In a Landscape of Having to Repeat* (Omnidawn, 2004), p.84.

Maggie Nelson's *The Argonauts* (Graywolf, 2016) is the source of the Section II epigraph, p. 96, paperback edition.

Section III's epigraph is from Emily Dickinson's well-known poem #1463, beginning "A Route of Evanescence..." *The Complete Poems of Emily Dickinson,* ed. Thomas H. Johnson (Little Brown, 1960), p. 619.

Section IV opens with an epigraph quoted from Mary Oliver's poem "Wild Geese," from *Dreamwork* (Atlantic Monthly Press, 1986).

"Dry Arroyos" owes a debt to Lewis Turco and his terzanelle "Thunder Weather."

The "Meanwhile" prose poems in Sections I, II, and IV are inspired by autobiographical sketches recording boyhood experiences at the turn of the 20th century—these preserved in a notebook from my father. In spirit and in form, the poems owe a debt also to Jean Follain's *A World Rich in Anniversaries,* published in *Dreaming the Miracle: Three French Prose Poets,* tr. Mary Feeney and William Matthews (White Pine, 2003), pp. 165-206. Follain was my father's chronological contemporary.

"Cochineal" makes reference to the cultural history of red dye, a more brilliant and saturated hue than had been available to Western traders and artisans until it was found in the dried bodies of female parasitic insects living on nopal cacti in Mexico.

"To the Piano" shows the influence of Pablo Neruda's odes, in particular those published in *Full Woman, Fleshly Apple, Hot Moon: Selected Poems of Pablo Neruda,* tr. Stephen Mitchell (HarperCollins, 1997).

"Eating and Other Disorders" and "The Whole Stock" are based on Raymond Queneau: his sonnet grid, *Cent Mille Milliards de Poemes,* as presented in their original and in English translation by Beverly Charles Rowe. The grid features poems intended for use as palimpsests. Sonnets 3 and 9 were the bases for the sonnets appearing here.

In "Hosting the Duke at the Cotton Club," the texts of stanzas 1 and 4 follow closely the emcee's monologue heard on the 78-rpm recording "A Night at the Cotton Club, Part 2" featuring Duke Ellington and his Cotton Club Orchestra (RCA Victor, 1929).

"Barn Raising" takes a cue from "Food for a Barn Raising," a list found in Mary Emma Showalter's *Mennonite Community Cookbook* (Scottsdale, PA: The Mennonite Community Association, 1957), p. 54.

John Rushworth Jellicoe, mentioned in "Meanwhile: Mimes & Ghosts, Part 1," was a well-known British naval officer during World War I.

Acknowledgments

I am grateful to the editors of the following publications for giving these poems a home, sometimes in earlier incarnations or with different titles.

Askew: "Elegance"
The Centrifugal Eye: "Traveling Alone in Assisi"
The Chickasaw Plum: "Barn Raising"
The Comstock Review: "To Another Guest, After the Wedding"
The Dirty Napkin: "The Legs for It," "I Read into David Hockney's Painting"
Flyway: "For Girlhood"
The Foundling Review: "Migration"
Inlandia: "Cochineal," "Chalcedony," "Frankincense," "Conversation at Night," "Of Petrarch and Cigarettes"
Innisfree: "In Your Midnight Kitchen" and "Cooking with Garlic," as sections of "The Garlic Peelers"; "On Being Here"
Mason's Road: "To the Piano"
Mid-American Review: "Meanwhile: Visions & Dreams," Parts 2 and 3; "Occasions & Notions," Part 2; "Mimes & Ghosts," Part 2 as sections of "Earth Beneath the Snow."
Midwest Quarterly: "Steelies," "Prairie Madness"
Moria: "Apologia for Prayer"
New Verse News: "Some Words for Meanwhile"
Poemeleon: "Dry Arroyos," "Bunting with Birders"
The Prose-Poem Project: "Meanwhile: Occasions & Notions," Part 1; "Mimes & Ghosts," Part 1
Psychic Meatloaf: "Impromptus on the Figure of a Fan"
qaartsiluni: "Eating and Other Disorders"
Red River Review: "Something in Me Wanting to Be Bad"
Rufous City Review: "Love's Supper"
The Sow's Ear: "Toes in the Grass," "Homage to Style," "Extra"
Stirring: "Meanwhile: Visions & Dreams," Part 1; "Occasions & Notions," Part 3
Tar River Poetry: "When Warhol Sat for Alice Neel"
Untitled Country Review: "Hosting the Duke at the Cotton Club," "Ten Miles from Home"

"Toes in the Grass" (as "Open to the Elements") was a prize winner in *Rhyme Zone's 2014-15 Poetry Competition* and appeared on the Rhyme Zone blog spot.

The poem "Tomatoes" first appeared (as "Dinner After the Storm") in *Element(ary), My Dear* (Kind of a Hurricane Press, 2016).

"Turquoise" first appeared in *Thirty Days: Best of the 30/30 Project's First Year* (Tupelo Press, 2015).

A host of mentors and poets have surrounded me on the way to making this book a reality. Deep thanks to Judith Terzi, Frances McConnel, and Richard Garcia, whose agile attention to many poem drafts through the years has strengthened the poet in me. Thanks to Linda Dove and Stephen Webber, who read this manuscript at earlier stages and offered gracious insight, as well as to Lois P. Jones, whose reading of the collection was the basis for her radio conversation with me on KPFK's Poet's Café. Special thanks to Joan Houlihan and my cohort at her 2017 Colrain Conference for their keen advice; and to Tupelo Press and Jeffrey Levine, whose Bay Area weekend conferences made such a vital difference.

Thanks are due to so many others who have encouraged me with their support through the gestation and harvest of this book. To each of the following, I'm grateful for your engagement and your company along this winding path: Karen Greenbaum-Maya and Genevieve Kaplan, co-conspirators along with Frances McConnel of Fourth Sundays Poetry; Riverside poets Lavina Blossom, Charlotte Davidson, Judy Kronenfeld, and Cati Porter. It's my great pleasure to thank Marsha de la O, Jeffrey Levine, and Richard Garcia for their cover blurbs and Diane Kistner for her insight, wisdom, and skill in creating a work of art from my collection of poems.

The forbearance and understanding of my husband John has been crucial, as well as that of my daughters and their spouses. To their love I owe much!

About FutureCycle Press

FutureCycle Press is dedicated to publishing lasting English-language poetry books, chapbooks, and anthologies in both print-on-demand and Kindle ebook formats. Founded in 2007 by long-time independent editor/publishers and partners Diane Kistner and Robert S. King, the press incorporated as a nonprofit in 2012. A number of our editors are distinguished poets and writers in their own right, and we have been actively involved in the small press movement going back to the early seventies.

The FutureCycle Poetry Book Prize and honorarium is awarded annually for the best full-length volume of poetry we publish in a calendar year. Introduced in 2013, our Good Works projects are anthologies devoted to issues of universal significance, with all proceeds donated to a related worthy cause. Our Selected Poems series highlights contemporary poets with a substantial body of work to their credit; with this series we strive to resurrect work that has had limited distribution and is now out of print.

We are dedicated to giving all of the authors we publish the care their work deserves, making our catalog of titles the most diverse and distinguished it can be, and paying forward any earnings to fund more great books.

We've learned a few things about independent publishing over the years. We've also evolved a unique, resilient publishing model that allows us to focus mainly on vetting and preserving for posterity poetry collections of exceptional quality without becoming overwhelmed with bookkeeping and mailing, fundraising activities, or taxing editorial and production "bubbles." To find out more about what we are doing, come see us at www.futurecycle.org.

The FutureCycle Poetry Book Prize

All full-length volumes of poetry published by FutureCycle Press in a given calendar year are considered for the annual FutureCycle Poetry Book Prize. This allows us to consider each submission on its own merits, outside of the context of a contest. Too, the judges see the finished book, which will have benefitted from the beautiful book design and strong editorial gloss we are famous for.

The book ranked the best in judging is announced as the prize-winner in the subsequent year. There is no fixed monetary award; instead, the winning poet receives an honorarium of 20% of the total net royalties from all poetry books and chapbooks the press sold on-line in the year the winning book was published. The winner is also accorded the honor of being on the panel of judges for the next year's competition; all judges receive copies of all contending books to keep for their personal library.

www.ingramcontent.com/pod-product-compliance
Lightning Source LLC
Chambersburg PA
CBHW070007100426
42741CB00012B/3145